W9-BVL-302

COUNTDOWN TO SPACE

LIVING ON MARS
Mission to the Red Planet

Michael D. Cole

Series Advisor:
John E. McLeaish
Chief, Public Information Office, retired,
NASA Johnson Space Center

Enslow Publishers, Inc.

40 Industrial Road   PO Box 38
Box 398   Aldershot
Berkeley Heights, NJ 07922 Hants GU12 6BP
USA   UK

http://www.enslow.com

Library of Congress Cataloging-in-Publication Data

Cole, Michael D.
    Living on Mars : mission to the Red Planet / Michael D. Cole.
        p.   cm. — (Countdown to space)
    Includes bibliographical references and index.
    Summary: Describes the landing of Sojourner on Mars, summarizes the
history of information gathering missions, and speculates about future
plans for explorations of the Red Planet.
    ISBN: 0-7660-1121-6
    1. Space flight to Mars—Juvenile literature. 2. Mars (Planet)—Exploration—
Juvenile literature. [1. Space flight to Mars. 2. Mars (Planet)] I. Title.
II. Series.
TL799.M3C63   1999
919.9' 23' 04—dc21   98-13125
                                                            CIP
                                                             AC

Printed in the United States of America

10 9 8 7 6 5 4 3

To Our Readers: We have done our best to make sure all Internet addresses in this
book were active and appropriate when we went to press. However, the author and
the publisher have no control over and assume no liability for the material available
on those Internet sites or on other Web sites they may link to. Any comments or
suggestions can be sent by e-mail to comments@enslow.com or to the address on the
back cover.

Illustration Credits: National Aeronautics and Space Administration
(NASA).

Cover Illustration: NASA (foreground); Raghvendra Sahai and John
Trauger (JPL), the WFPC2 science team, NASA, and AURA/STSCI
(background).

Cover Photo: An artist's depiction of a future landing on Mars.

CONTENTS

In the twenty-first century, the National Aeronautics and Space Administration (NASA) hopes to send humans on the first manned journey to Mars.

1

First Martian Driver

On July 4, 1997, the United States' *Pathfinder* spacecraft landed on the dusty red surface of the planet Mars. It had taken seven months for the unmanned spacecraft to travel to the planet.

The landing had been cushioned by large balloons, which had inflated all around the spacecraft to protect it. Soon after landing, the balloons gently deflated and *Pathfinder* settled solidly to the surface. With *Pathfinder* successfully landed, the next part of the mission was about to begin. It was time for *Pathfinder* to open its doors and release its small robotic vehicle, *Sojourner*. *Sojourner* was a rover equipped with cameras and scientific equipment. It would analyze the soil, rocks, and atmosphere of Mars.

Everything was ready with the little rover. From the top of its solar panels to the bottom of its six metal wheels, *Sojourner* was not much larger than a microwave oven. The robotic machine slowly rolled down a ramp and out onto the Martian soil. At the controls of *Sojourner,* millions of miles away on Earth, was Brian Cooper.

Cooper worked at the Jet Propulsion Laboratory (JPL), which is part of the National Aeronautics and Space Administration (NASA). JPL is where most of NASA's space probes to other planets are controlled. Cooper operated *Sojourner* by computer and a set of visual goggles. JPL, in Pasadena, California, is not far from where Cooper grew up in Torrance, California.

Not surprisingly, Brian's favorite things when he was growing up were remote-control cars. As he got older, he grew to love the early computer games like Space Invaders and Pac-Man. In 1969, when Brian was only nine years old, he was amazed to watch Neil Armstrong walk on the Moon.

"How neat is that?" he was always saying.[1]

The Moon missions made him want to become a pilot, or even an astronaut. When Cooper went to college, he joined the Air Force and went through school as an Air Force cadet. He then learned that his eyesight was too bad to ever become a pilot. He was very disappointed. But Cooper's interest in robots and machines would get him far beyond the Moon in another way.

The Pathfinder *spacecraft parachutes to a landing on the dusty red landscape of Mars. Its landing is cushioned by the large balloons.*

"I built my first robot in college," said Cooper, who earned a degree in electrical engineering. "I used it to explore my living room."[2]

When Cooper began working at JPL, he was first part of the team monitoring the *Voyager* spacecraft, which was on its way to Jupiter. Then he began developing and testing robotic vehicles. His work eventually led to the design and construction of *Sojourner*.

"This is what I wanted to do since I came to the Jet Propulsion Laboratory," Cooper said. "I've always had a fascination for things you can control."

Cooper's wife looked at it another way. "He basically built his own video game," she said. "Now he's playing it."[3]

The greatest challenge of controlling *Sojourner* on Mars was the distance between Earth and Mars. It took eleven minutes for Cooper's electronic signals to travel through space and reach the rover on Mars. This also meant that television images of Mars from the rover would take eleven minutes to travel back to Cooper.

"If I were to see a cliff on my computer screen and tell the rover to stop, it would have fallen off by the time my signal got there," Cooper explained.[4] For this reason, all movements of the rover were done very carefully, in stages. The *Pathfinder* lander took pictures all around the rover and sent them by radio signal to Earth. Cooper then studied the pictures, which were displayed in 3-D on a computer screen.

"I can see the surface of Mars as if I'm standing there," he said. "I can sense depth. I can see how far away

Technicians at the Kennedy Space Center inspect the Sojourner *rover before its mission to Mars.*

the rocks are." When Cooper and his team decided where they wanted the rover to go, Cooper sent his commands to the lander, which relayed them to *Sojourner*. Eleven minutes later, the rover began to execute Cooper's list of electronic commands, moving at a slow pace of two feet per minute. "I'll be performing my functions while the rover is asleep," Cooper said. "Then I'll come home and sleep while the rover is driving."[5]

Sojourner was used to analyze the chemistry of Martian soil and rocks. The little rover and the *Pathfinder* spacecraft that carried it were sent to help scientists learn whether there had ever been life on Mars. Scientists did not expect to find signs that there had ever been advanced forms of life like the animals and humans on Earth. But the landscape of Mars shows many plains and channels that suggest the planet at some time had water flowing on the surface. Some scientists think that Mars was once partially covered with oceans. It is possible that microscopic organisms may have existed in these oceans or along their shorelines millions of years ago.

If life did once exist on Mars, some people believe there will be ways to have life exist there again. To do this, it will take a little help from the people on Mars' nearest planet, Earth.

Pathfinder and *Sojourner* were the early steps on a journey that may someday lead to human beings living on Mars. If human beings ever branch out to live on other worlds, Mars is the first planet where it will happen.

If you are young, you will probably live to see the first astronauts walk upon Mars. Perhaps you will even be one of them. Mars is a goal for human space exploration for many reasons. It is one of our nearest planets, and it is reachable by our current methods of space travel. Of all the planets in our solar system, Mars is the most like Earth.

The soil of Mars possesses a supply of water in the form of permafrost. Water also exists at the polar ice caps, and more may be hidden deep underground. The planet's soil is rich in carbon, nitrogen, hydrogen, and oxygen. Humans need a supply of these four elements to survive.

We already have the technology to send people to Mars. But planning such a mission requires a tremendous effort. The cost of designing and building the spacecraft that would carry people to Mars and back to Earth will be huge. Building the equipment and training the people who would go to Mars will cost the countries involved many billions of dollars.

Because the public pays for the space program, the public must be in support of any space project. When the time is right, the space program will have to turn the public's attention toward Mars. It may not be too difficult, as Mars has captured people's imagination before.

There are three classes of Martian rocks that Sojourner analyzed. The first class (red arrow) has a weathered coating. The second class (blue arrows) is unweathered smaller rocks. The third class (white arrow) is exposed white material from several centimeters deep.

The public experienced a brief sort of Mars craze in the late 1800s. Using an early telescope, astronomer Percival Lowell saw what he believed to be canals on the surface of Mars. These canals, he speculated, had been built by a race of intelligent Martian beings. The canals and the beings who supposedly built them never existed, though. They were just fanciful explanations for what Lowell believed he saw through the imperfect lenses of his telescope.[6]

The Red Planet has had a special place in the imagination of our culture for a long time. The thought of finally sending astronauts to land and walk on Mars is something that many citizens around the world will find very exciting. Before anyone goes there, we must learn more about the planet Mars.

2

The Red Planet

The first astronauts to land on Mars will find themselves upon a very dry world. The only water that exists on the planet today is in its soil and at its polar ice caps, similar to the North and South Poles on Earth. Although Mars is much smaller than Earth, it has about the same amount of land surface, since much of Earth is covered by oceans.

Because Mars travels around the sun in an elliptical orbit, astronauts will experience tremendous shifts in the planet's temperature. An ellipse is a circle that is somewhat flattened, or egg-shaped. Although Earth's orbit is also elliptical, its orbit is more circular than Mars'. Earth stays at about the same distance from the sun at all times. Mars' elliptical orbit carries it closer to the sun at some parts of its year and farther away at others.

Temperatures as high as 70°F (21°C) have been recorded at one time of the year, and as low as –220°F (–140°C) at another time.[1] Whatever heat does manage to build up on Mars' surface escapes through the planet's very thin atmosphere soon after sunset.

Although there is some oxygen in the Martian atmosphere, humans will not be able to breathe on Mars. The atmosphere is mostly carbon dioxide, with only

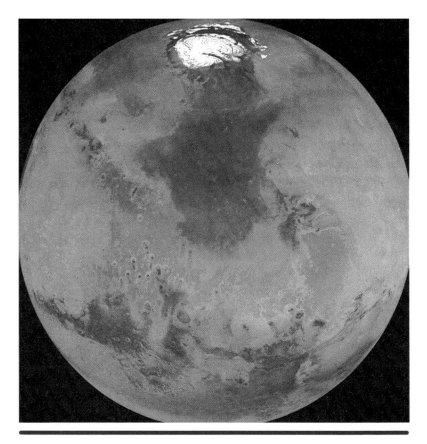

Water exists at the ice caps of Mars, seen here as the white area on the planet's polar region.

traces of oxygen and other gases. Without a thick atmosphere to hold in the heat from the day and with too little oxygen for humans to breathe, Mars will not be able to support humans unless they are protected. Astronauts will always need space suits on this planet to protect them from the cold and to supply their oxygen.[2]

Human visitors to Mars will walk upon the planet in a fashion similar to the way astronauts bounced around in the lighter gravity of the Moon, but not quite as much. The Moon has only one sixth the gravity of Earth. The gravity of Mars is a bit stronger, about one third the gravity of Earth.

Much of the soil these astronauts will be walking on is red. Mars is often referred to as the Red Planet. In Roman times, the planet was associated with the god of war because it was the color of blood. Much of the dusty landscape of Mars is red because it is experiencing a chemical reaction called oxidation. Simply put, the Martian surface is undergoing a process similar to what happens to metal when it is exposed to air for a long time. The surface of Mars, which contains some metals, is rusting.

When Mars' first human visitors look up from this dusty red soil and into the night sky, they will see the planet's two moons, Phobos and Deimos. Both of the moons are small, but Deimos is the smaller. It is only twenty miles across. It is not even round like our Moon, but looks more like a cratered rock. Phobos is slightly

Much of the surface of Mars is red because it is rusting.

larger and orbits closer to Mars. Because they are so small, neither Phobos nor Deimos would light up the night sky the way the Moon lights up the Earth on some clear nights.[3]

The first Earth spacecraft to reach Mars was the *Mariner 4* space probe in 1965. *Mariner 4* took pictures of the planet's surface and analyzed the various properties of its atmosphere. It was followed in 1969 by *Mariner 6* and *Mariner 7*, which made further studies of the Martian atmosphere as they flew past. *Mariner 9*, in 1971, was the first spacecraft to go into orbit around

Mars. It sent over seven thousand pictures back to Earth and mapped the entire surface of the planet.[4]

These first spacecraft, passing many miles above the planet, could neither prove nor disprove the existence of life on Mars. The next step was to land a probe on the planet to study it close-up.

On July 20, 1976, *Viking 1* successfully landed on Mars. A robotic arm reached out and grasped a scoop of soil. It pulled it back inside the lander, and a number of scientific instruments analyzed the properties of the soil. Despite the various tests conducted at both the *Viking 1* and *Viking 2* landing sites, scientists could not say for certain whether or not life existed on Mars. More tests and more exploration of the planet needed to be done.

The Hubble Space Telescope, which stays in orbit around Earth, has taken many pictures and conducted several studies of Mars since its launch in 1990. But following the Viking landings in 1976, twenty years passed before another spacecraft was launched from Earth toward Mars. Just months before the *Mars Global Surveyor* and *Pathfinder* were launched to Mars in November and December of 1996, something remarkable happened. A small meteorite that had been discovered in Antarctica in 1984 was now actually thought to be a piece of Mars.

Scientists conducted tests on this chunk of rock. Traces of chemicals within the meteorite showed possible evidence that life had once existed on Mars.

These six instruments carried aboard the Mars Global Surveyor *spacecraft took photographs, analyzed magnetic fields, and studied the atmosphere.*

NASA administrator Daniel Goldin made this announcement in August 1996:

> NASA has made a startling discovery that points to the possibility that a primitive form of microscopic life may have existed on Mars more than 3 billion years ago. I want everyone to understand that we are not talking about "little green men." These are extremely small, single-cell structures. . . . The evidence is exciting, even compelling, but not conclusive. It is a discovery that demands further scientific investigation.[5]

Four months later, the Mars *Pathfinder* lifted off from

Cape Canaveral, Florida. By July 4, 1997, it was descending through the thin atmosphere of Mars and inflating the balloons that would cushion its landing. Following the successful landing, Brian Cooper and the rover team at the Jet Propulsion Laboratory (JPL) rolled *Sojourner* out onto the Martian surface.

The JPL team carefully drove the rover up to a ten-inch-high rock, which they had named Barnacle Bill. To the scientists' surprise, *Sojourner*'s instruments indicated that Barnacle Bill was very similar to the melted, hardened, and remelted rocks found on Earth near active volcanoes. *Sojourner*'s analysis of Barnacle Bill

The launch of Pathfinder *began the next phase in the exciting exploration of Mars.*

suggested that the geology of Mars was far more complex than scientists had previously thought.

"It's not the easiest rock to make," said one NASA scientist, "and that alone is very exciting."[6]

The analysis also showed that Barnacle Bill's chemical makeup was similar but not identical to the Antarctic meteorite that was believed to be from Mars. *Sojourner* moved on to study other rocks, which the team named Scooby Doo, Yogi, Wedge, and Shark. Another rock that *Sojourner* photographed but did not analyze was named Casper because it appeared ghostly white in the photographs.

The next spacecraft to arrive in orbit around the planet was the *Mars Global Surveyor*. It spent a full Mars year, which is equal to almost two Earth years, mapping the planet in great detail. Other spacecraft will follow, doing further studies of Mars. One of these spacecraft is expected to land on Mars and lift off again to return a Martian soil sample to Earth for closer study. Sending a probe to Mars and having it return will also test the ability of a spacecraft to make such a trip. Before humans are sent to Mars, we must be confident that our spacecraft work well enough to bring them back again.

These robotic missions to the planet are yielding great amounts of knowledge. They are also moving us closer to the exciting day when we send the first astronauts to Mars.

3

Voyage to Another World

In the first or second decade of the twenty-first century, the people of Earth may witness one of the most historic journeys in human history—the first visit by human beings to another planet, Mars. The first human visit to Mars will not be like the short missions to the Moon by the Apollo astronauts. The cost of going to Mars is far too high to go there for only a brief time, collect some soil and rock samples, and come home.

Because of the great distance and the months that astronauts would spend traveling in space before they arrive at the planet, the journey to Mars will be a large expedition. The entire mission would take about three years, and the astronauts would be on the surface for as long as a year.

On a space journey of this kind, the astronauts must be prepared for anything. If something goes wrong, there is no way to hurry home across millions of miles! They must have many backups, or what the scientists at NASA call redundant systems, in case of equipment failure. They may have more than one spacecraft on the planet with which to return to Earth. The astronauts may set up more than one power-generating system on Mars so that the failure of one system will not mean total power failure for their equipment. Total power failure could mean danger or even death for the astronauts.

The astronauts would have to take along all the supplies and equipment they would need in order to deal with the problems they might encounter on that alien world. Although their activities would be monitored by scientists on Earth, with a five- to twenty-minute lag in communications, these first explorers of Mars would essentially be on their own.

In the late 1990s there was no official agreement on exactly how the first human missions to Mars would be conducted. Earlier in the decade, NASA envisioned a huge plan for going to Mars, which would not be attempted until after the International Space Station was completed and a permanent base was in place on the Moon.[1]

Designs for human missions to Mars changed later in the 1990s. Scientists began to see the importance of

The International Space Station, pictured here, will be completed before NASA attempts a manned mission to Mars.

using smaller spacecraft, possibly with the fuel for the return trip produced by a chemical reaction on the surface of Mars instead of carrying the fuel all the way from Earth.[2] The designs will probably continue to change as scientists learn more about the planet and the performance of the different robotic spacecraft traveling there.

Eventually the time will arrive to make that historic journey to Mars. It may proceed something like this:

Two years before the first crew is launched, a robotic Earth Return Vehicle (ERV) will be launched from Earth. It will arrive in orbit around Mars eight months later. The ERV will consist of three parts. The first part will be the fully fueled rocket engine that will power the spacecraft out of Mars orbit for its return to Earth. The second part will be the habitat module, in which the crew will live during its return trip from Mars. Atop this module will be a crew return capsule. When the ERV enters Earth orbit, the crew will climb into this capsule and separate it from the habitat module. The astronauts will use the crew return capsule, which is equipped with a heat shield, to reenter Earth's atmosphere and land on Earth.[3]

A second robotic launch will deliver the first cargo of equipment to the Mars landing site. The spacecraft that arrives on the planet with this mission will deliver the Mars Ascent Vehicle (MAV), which the astronauts will use to launch themselves back into space to the ERV when their stay on Mars is over. Also delivered will be a fuel production facility, a nuclear reactor mounted in the back of a robotic truck, a supply of liquid hydrogen, and forty tons of additional cargo and equipment that will eventually be used by the astronauts.[4]

Shortly after this spacecraft lands, the robotic truck with the nuclear reactor will be lowered to the Martian surface. Similar to the way *Pathfinder* was controlled from Earth, the robotic truck will be driven several hundred yards away from the spacecraft. Next, the fuel production facility will be deployed and driven a short distance away. The nuclear reactor will then begin to provide power to the fuel production facility.

Inside the fuel facility, a chemical reaction will occur between a supply of hydrogen brought from Earth and the carbon dioxide gas in the Martian atmosphere. The reaction will produce oxygen and methane fuel that the MAV will use to launch the crew back into space. The rest of the fuel will be used in the astronauts' Mars rovers.[5]

The white triangular Mars Ascent Vehicle will launch astronauts from Mars' surface to the Earth Return Vehicle orbiting the Red Planet.

The facility will also produce additional amounts of oxygen for the astronauts' breathing. Water will be produced by combining the oxygen with the hydrogen brought from Earth.

A third robotic mission will launch a surface habitat module to Mars. The astronauts who first land on Mars will make this module their home. The habitat module will land in the same area as the MAV, the nuclear reactor, and the fuel facility. A second nuclear reactor will also be delivered, which will be driven out to

When astronauts land on Mars, they will need to stay there for up to a year. During their stay, the astronauts will live in habitation modules similar to the ones pictured here.

the area near the first reactor. Thus, there will be two power systems available at the landing site. Each one of the reactors will be capable of producing all the energy that will be needed at the manned Mars outpost.

Two years after these three spacecraft have been launched, the process will begin again. Another ERV will be launched and put into orbit around Mars in case the first ERV fails. Another MAV will be landed on the planet's surface, with additional supplies and scientific equipment. This will be the last robotic spacecraft to land in preparation for the arrival of the first astronauts on Mars.[6]

Finally, the historic day will come. The first Mars crew of six astronauts will suit up and be driven to the launch complex, where their spacecraft will await them on the pad. The main part of their spacecraft will be a habitat module almost identical to the other habitat module already waiting for them on Mars.

This crew of astronauts will be going on the farthest journey any human beings have ever traveled. They will have said good-bye to their families. They will not see them again for nearly two and a half years. Despite all the exhaustive planning and preparation, problems could still occur. On a journey through space such as this, the dangers can never be completely eliminated.

Their spacecraft could be struck by a passing meteor or collide with a small uncharted asteroid. A fire could

The Mars Ascent Vehicle will carry astronauts from Mars to the larger Earth Return Vehicle.

break out and threaten everyone on board. It could even destroy the entire spacecraft.

Any number of mechanical failures might threaten to end the Mars mission before it ever reaches the planet. A failure with the engines could cause the astronauts to miss their rendezvous with Mars and send them drifting helplessly through space, until their supplies of food and oxygen gradually run out.

An astronaut may be badly injured or even killed while working on the surface of Mars. If a space suit is torn and depressurizes while the astronauts are far from the habitat modules, that astronaut could run out of oxygen and die long before reaching the habitat's pressurized airlock.

Like every astronaut before them has understood, these travelers will know there is a possibility they may never see their families again.

But they are ready. The countdown proceeds. Weather around the launch area is good. All systems on the spacecraft are go. The time has come; the countdown ticks toward its final moments.

Ten . . . nine . . . eight . . . seven . . . six . . . five . . . four . . . three . . . two . . . one . . . Ignition. Liftoff!

The spacecraft roars off the pad and into the sky toward space. A few minutes later the crew is in orbit around Earth. The first stage of their rocket drops away. The astronauts prepare for the firing of the second stage rocket. When the second stage engine fires, the spacecraft is pushed out of Earth orbit on a path that will intersect with Mars. Depending on when their mission begins, the spacecraft will arrive at Mars between 120 and 180 days later.[7]

Once they are out of Earth orbit and the engines push the spacecraft to its top speed, there is no turning back. They are bound for Mars.

During the long journey toward the planet, the crew is kept busy conducting a variety of scientific experiments. Their days in the spacecraft are similar to the days that astronauts have spent aboard the space shuttle. They work, eat, rest, and have a little time for relaxation. The crew's time aboard the spacecraft during the Mars flight will be about the same period that many astronauts have spent aboard the Russian *Mir* space station. By the time of this first Mars mission, astronauts will have spent similar amounts of time aboard the International Space Station.

The astronauts will also need to keep in shape during

the flight. Although the gravity of Mars is only about one third the gravity of Earth, the crew members will still need strong bodies to conduct their work when they arrive on the planet. An exercise bike and treadmill are the primary equipment astronauts will use to keep their leg muscles strong while in space.

Toward the end of their flight, the astronauts watch the dusty red globe of Mars grow larger and larger out their spacecraft's windows. They are getting ever nearer to the alien world.

It is time to slow the spacecraft and lock carefully into orbit around the planet. After achieving orbit, the spacecraft is slowed even further, allowing the Martian gravity to pull the spacecraft out of orbit and closer to-

ward its surface. Strapping themselves in, the astronauts prepare for the landing sequence.

As they descend through the thin Martian atmosphere, the landing rockets ignite to slow the spacecraft's descent. The astronauts listen in their helmets as the spacecraft's radio picks up the sound of a

After months of travel, the astronauts will be able to see the Red Planet.

Streaking across the sky, the astronauts begin the descent into the Martian atmosphere.

beacon from the landing site. The homing beacon, transmitted by equipment already at the site, helps guide the spacecraft over the Martian landscape toward the landing location.[8]

To the astronauts who can see out the windows, the hills and valleys of Mars no longer look like features on a map. They are now three-dimensional and crisply detailed. The shadows of hills and individual rocks can be seen as the spacecraft passes over the planet. The beacon signals the commander that the landing site is near.

Suddenly it comes into view. The spacecraft is slowed even more. The cargo vehicles and the other habitat module are visible in the distance. Hovering a few more seconds, the spacecraft gently descends the last few feet toward the surface. Red Martian soil is kicked up in dusty clouds by the thrust from the descent engine.

All at once there is a jolt.

The landing legs have touched down on the surface. The descent engine stops. After months in space, all is suddenly still.

The crew members eagerly unbuckle their harnesses. They rise and look out the windows at the strange alien world that will be their home for about the next year. They will probably stand there looking for a long time.

They are the first human beings to land on Mars.

4

Astronauts on Mars

The astronauts might find it a little comforting to see the fully fueled MAV and the other parts of their outpost already in place. But the rest of their view will be quite alien. They will not be used to the color of the soil, which almost everywhere on Mars has a definite rusty redness. The air is so thin that there will be no blue sky or puffy clouds like they will have known on Earth. The red dust floating in the air will leave the color of the sky changing only from shades of pink to shades of orange.

The hatch on the crew's habitat module opens, and the first space-suited astronaut descends the ladder. In a few moments, the astronaut moves off the ladder and takes the first human steps on another planet. This astronaut will probably pause to say a few brief words about the historic accomplishment, as Neil Armstrong did when he first stepped on the Moon and said, "That's one small step for a man, one giant leap for mankind."

Next, the astronaut walks away from the habitat module, testing how the suit and equipment feel in the Martian gravity. Other crew members follow onto the surface. They may conduct a small ceremony and perhaps erect a flag or plaque that represents the people of Earth.

Then it is time to get to work. The astronauts unpack cargo, assemble and test their rovers, and check on the operation of the fuel production facility and both nuclear

After landing on Mars, the crew uses a rover to unload cargo.

reactors. For the next six to twelve months, the crew members explore Mars for miles around their landing site, conducting a wide range of scientific experiments.

The main purpose of this first manned mission to Mars is to have humans available to help in discovering whether life has ever existed on Mars. Understanding the planet and its history will help us better understand how life may have existed and evolved on the planet. Such knowledge will ultimately help scientists to understand how existing forms of life on Earth might be adapted and introduced into the Martian environment. When this is accomplished, human beings may be able to live on Mars and, perhaps, on other planets.[1]

The astronauts explore many miles of the surface to conduct investigations about the planet's geology. Their cargo includes a large drill that can dig deep into the planet's crust to take samples of its soil and rock.[2] They set up weather stations and meteorologic equipment to observe the Martian atmosphere.

Robotic rovers are driven a few miles away to make observations. The crew members operate them by watching the view from the television camera aboard the rover. Since there is no communication lag time, the astronaut in the habitat module can control the rover as if he or she were actually on it. If something very interesting or important is discovered by the rover, a team of astronauts can go to the site to investigate it further.

The completed outpost on Mars includes the crew's two-story lander habitat (left) and inflatable laboratory (right). A Mars Ascent Vehicle can be seen in the distance.

Another kind of rover is driven by the astronauts and is powered by the chemical fuel created in the fuel production facility. With the fuel available from this facility, astronauts can travel a total of 14,000 miles in these rovers by the end of their stay on the planet. This mileage gives them a great deal of mobility in accomplishing their exploration tasks.[3]

The astronauts also construct a greenhouse at the landing site. Inside the greenhouse, various plants are grown to test their ability to adapt to the alien conditions on Mars. Learning about ways to grow plants and foods on the planet is very important if humans are ever to live permanently on Mars.

After about a year of experiments and exploration on the planet, it is time for the first crew of astronauts to leave their outpost on Mars. Their cargo of equipment and scientific samples is loaded aboard the MAV. All six astronauts climb aboard the MAV and prepare for liftoff.

By this time, the fully fueled MAV has been sitting at the Martian landing site for nearly four years. The crew checks out all its flight systems to make sure they are ready for the launch. When all systems are go, they prepare for liftoff, hoping that everything will work.

Again there is a countdown. *Five . . . four . . . three . . . two . . . one . . . zero!*

At *zero* the crew members feel their bodies pushed toward the floor as the MAV launches them rapidly from the landing site. Gaining speed, the MAV soars through the thin, pinkish atmosphere of Mars. Several minutes after launch the astronauts are once again in orbit around the planet. Their next task is to dock with the ERV, which was the first of the Mars mission vehicles to arrive in orbit around the planet. It has been there for four years.

Maneuvering into position, the crew successfully docks with the ERV. After docking, the astronauts transfer themselves and their cargo of equipment, supplies, and scientific samples from the MAV to the

ERV. Once the crew is secure in the ERV and the hatch between the two spacecraft is sealed, an astronaut pulls a lever that allows the MAV to separate from the ERV. The MAV then drifts away, eventually crashing to the surface of Mars.

The crew gets the ERV ready for the long engine burn that will boost them away from Mars orbit and send them on their way back to Earth. At precisely the right moment, the engines are switched on. The crew members feel themselves gradually pressed backward. When the engines switch off, their instruments confirm

The Mars Ascent Vehicle blasts the crew members from the surface of Mars. It will then dock with the Earth Return Vehicle that orbits Mars.

that the ERV has broken away from Mars orbit. They are headed home.

The crew compartment of the ERV is a habitat module similar to the ones that carried them to Mars and in which they lived on the planet's surface.[4] The journey back to Earth in the ERV is very much like the outbound trip to Mars.

The crew has now been in a reduced gravity environment for nearly two years. Low gravity over long periods causes the astronauts' bones to lose calcium and weaken. They must exercise very hard during their return trip to keep their bones from becoming too weak. They will need strong bones to stand and walk in normal gravity when they get back to Earth.

About five months later, the astronauts look out their windows. The beautiful blue sphere of Earth grows larger and larger with every hour. If this first Mars crew is like the astronauts who returned from the Moon, they will have gained a new appreciation for their home world, a planet so rich with life.

The ERV then comes into orbit around Earth. The crew members transfer themselves and their cargo of scientific samples from the ERV's habitat module to the reentry capsule. When the command is given, the capsule separates from the habitat module, and the crew begins to descend through Earth's atmosphere. The blunt end of the capsule is a heat shield that protects the capsule from the intense heat caused by friction with the atmosphere.

Once the capsule is through the upper atmosphere, it continues to fall. Parachutes deploy from the capsule moments later, slowing its descent toward an open area of land, where a recovery team is waiting. Descending with the parachutes, the capsule with the first Mars crew drifts down on the winds toward a final and triumphant return to Earth.

After spending about two years away from home, the crew parachutes to a landing. It is a great ending to their successful mission.

The first human beings have traveled to Mars . . . and back.

It does not end there. Not long after this first crew has returned, a second crew is launched on another long journey to Mars. More surface habitats and more nuclear reactors have gone ahead of them. It has become a successful system, and the Martian outpost grows.[5] When these outposts gradually evolve into settlements, the planet Mars will become the New World of the twenty-first century. It will be a great accomplishment.

Even if no evidence is found of life ever having existed on Mars, the Red Planet still promises to play an important role in the future of humans in space. Someday the people working in these Mars settlements, far from the blue skies of Earth, may answer many questions about the existence of life on other planets. Someday these settlers' answer to whether there is life on Mars may, in fact, depend on what sort of life is being asked about. These settlers might answer that they are the life on Mars.

Just think. One day, fifty to one hundred years from now, there may be a whole group of people who were born under the red and dusty sky of Mars. Although they are our fellow humans, they may feel a little different about themselves. It is possible that this new and unique generation of people may proudly and accurately wish to refer to themselves as Martians.

CHAPTER NOTES

Chapter 1. First Martian Driver

1. British Broadcasting Company, "Brian Cooper—*Pathfinder Rover Driver*," *The Mars Files:* Pathfinder *Profiles*, June 1997, <http://www.bbc.co.uk/science/mars/Prof3.htm> (June 4, 1998).

2. Jeff Schnaufer, "Drive, He Says," *People Weekly*, July 21, 1997, p. 55.

3. Ibid.

4. Ibid.

5. Ibid.

6. Patrick Moore, *Travellers in Space and Time* (New York: Doubleday and Company, Inc., 1984), p. 43.

Chapter 2. The Red Planet

1. Dr. David R. Williams, "Mars Fact Sheet," *NSSDC Planetary Home Page*, January 29, 1998, <http://nssdc.gsfc.nasa.gov/planetary/factsheet/marsfact.html> (June 4, 1998).

2. Ibid.

3. Patrick Moore, *Travellers in Space and Time* (New York: Doubleday and Company, Inc., 1984), p. 44.

4. John and Nancy Dewaard, *History of NASA: America's Voyage to the Stars* (Greenwich, Conn.: Brompton, 1984), pp. 116–117.

5. Daniel S. Goldin, "Statement of Daniel S. Goldin, NASA Administrator," *NASA Press Releases 1996 Page*, August 6, 1996. <http://www.nasa.gov/releases/1996/> (June 5, 1998).

6. Leon Jerhoff, "Rock Festival on Mars," *Time*, vol. 150, no. 3, July 21, 1997, p. 55.

Chapter 3. Voyage to Another World

1. David Weaver, Michael Duke, and the American Institute of Aeronautics and Astronautics, "Mars Exploration Strategies: A Reference Program and Comparison of Alternative Architectures," *JSC Planetary Missions and Materials Exploration Server*, 1993, <http://www-sn.jsc.nasa.gov/explore/Data/Lib/DOCS/EIC043.HTML> (June 4, 1998).

2. Robert Zubrin, "The Promise of Mars," *Ad Astra*, May/June 1996, p. 34.

3. David Weaver, Michael Duke, Barney B. Roberts, and the American Institute of Aeronautics and Astronautics, "Mars Exploration Strategies: A Reference Design Mission," *JSC Planetary Missions and Materials Exploration Server*, 1993, <http://www-sn.jsc.nasa.gov/explore/Data/Lib/DOCS/EIC044.HTML> (June 4, 1998).

4. Ibid.

5. Zubrin, p. 33.

6. Weaver and Duke, *A Reference Design Mission*.

7. Weaver and Duke, *Alternative Architectures*.

8. Zubrin, p. 34.

Chapter 4. Astronauts on Mars

1. David Weaver, Michael Duke, and the American Institute of Aeronautics and Astronautics, "Mars Exploration Strategies: A Reference Program and Comparison of Alternative Architectures," *JSC Planetary Missions and Materials Exploration Server*, 1993, <http://www-sn.jsc.nasa.gov/explore/Data/Lib/DOCS/EIC043.HTML> (June 4, 1998).

2. Ibid.

3. Robert Zubrin, "The Promise of Mars," *Ad Astra*, May/June 1996, p. 34.

4. David Weaver, Michael Duke, Barney B. Roberts, and the American Institute of Aeronautics and Astronautics, "Mars Exploration Strategies: A Reference Design Mission," *JSC Planetary Missions and Materials Exploration Server*, 1993, <http://www-sn.jsc.nasa.gov/explore/Data/Lib/DOCS/EIC044.HTML> (June 4, 1998).

5. Weaver and Duke, *Alternative Architectures*.

GLOSSARY

deploy—To move an object into position.

Earth Return Vehicle (ERV)—The spacecraft that NASA envisions will return astronauts to Earth from Mars. It consists of an engine, a habitat module, and an Earth reentry capsule.

elliptical orbit—A path that is oval, or not quite circular.

heat shield—A layer that protects a space capsule from the intense heat caused by friction with the atmosphere.

Hubble Space Telescope—An orbiting observatory equipped with a very powerful telescope, designed to view objects up to 13 billion light-years away.

International Space Station—A permanent laboratory orbiting Earth that will enable us to conduct long-term research in space. It is the largest international scientific project ever attempted.

Mars Ascent Vehicle (MAV)—The spacecraft that NASA envisions will launch Mars astronauts back into orbit after their stay on the surface. It consists of a descent stage to land it on the planet, an ascent stage to lift it back into orbit, a cargo area, and a crew compartment.

Mars Global Surveyor—The NASA spacecraft launched in November 1996 that spent two years in Mars orbit mapping the entire surface of the planet.

meteorite—A piece of rock or debris from space that reaches the surface of Earth without being burned up completely in the atmosphere.

nuclear reactor—A power plant that uses the breakdown of atomic particles to produce electrical energy.

orbit—The path of one celestial body or spacecraft around another.

oxidation—The process of combining substances with oxygen. When iron and other metals are exposed to oxygen for long periods, the metals rust, or become oxidized.

NASA—The National Aeronautics and Space Administration, created in 1958.

Pathfinder—The NASA spacecraft that landed on Mars on July 4, 1997, releasing the *Sojourner* robotic rover to study Martian soil and rocks.

permafrost—A permanently frozen layer of ice beneath a frigid area of a planet's surface.

rendezvous—A meeting, such as when two spacecraft closely approach each other.

Sojourner—The robotic vehicle or rover that was released onto the Martian surface from the *Pathfinder* lander on July 4, 1997. *Sojourner*, controlled by computer from Earth, spent about five months studying Martian soil and rocks.

space shuttle—The first reusable spacecraft that carries astronauts and equipment into orbit; designed with wings so it can glide back to Earth.

FURTHER READING

Books

Corrick, James A. *Mars.* New York: Franklin Watts, Inc., 1991.

Desomma, Vincent. *The Mission to Mars and Beyond.* New York: Chelsea House, 1992.

Getz, David. *Life on Mars.* New York: Henry Holt & Co., Inc., 1997.

Hawkes, Nigel. *The New Book of Mars.* Brookfield, Conn.: Millbrook Press, Inc., 1998.

Kelch, Joseph W. *Millions of Miles to Mars: A Journey to the Red Planet.* Parsippany, N.J.: Julian Messner, 1995.

Landau, Elaine. *Mars.* Danbury, Conn.: Franklin Watts, Inc., 1991.

Schraff, Anne E. *Are We Moving to Mars?* Santa Fe, N.M.: John Muir Publications, 1996.

Zubrin, Robert. *The Case for Mars: The Plan to Settle the Red Planet and Why We Must.* New York: The Free Press, 1996.

Internet Sources

JPL. *Mars Missions, Year 2000 and Beyond.* n.d. <http://mpfwww.jpl.nasa.gov/> (April 17, 2000).

NASA/JPL. *Mars Pathfinder.* May 1, 1998. <http://mars.jpl.nasa.gov/MPF/index1.html> (April 17, 2000).

NASA's Quest Project. *Mars Team Online Home Page.* n.d. <http://quest.arc.nasa.gov/mars> (April 17, 2000).

INDEX